This ruled notebook is made for women and our allies. Nu is the pronunciation of "女", the Chinese word for woman. nu rule represents the modern movement for female empowerment. By leading in offices, classrooms, governments, and beyond, we are establishing a new rule.

A portion of the proceeds from every notebook is donated to nonprofits helping empower women. Thank you for supporting us as we lift each other up to succeed together.

Made in the USA
Middletown, DE
27 January 2020